Happy

in

My Blue Heaven

Happy in My Blue Heaven

Nora M. Corey, MHt., CRt.

ISBN 978-1-4116-6245-2

.

Dedication

I would like to express my heartfelt thanks to the people who have blessed my life. My sister, Jean, is my best friend, hero, and role model. I will always be grateful for her continued belief, pride, and support. My son John, who was spiritual before I knew the meaning of the word, has shown patience, guidance, and willingness to accompany me on my journey. My son James and brother Bob humored me even though they didn't always understand what I was talking about.

Each of you has been my light and my inspiration.

God Bless You.

Contents

Introduction

I awoke from sleep in the grip of terror. What had awakened me? A beam of moonlight invading the darkness through curtainless windows transformed familiar shapes into menacing shadow. The closed bedroom door muffled conversation from the living room below.

Eyes clamped tightly shut, I lay in a fetal position under heavy blankets mimicking the safety of a mother's womb. My breathing was shallow and sparse, the air heavy and stale. My mind raced, telling my body that if I lay perfectly still I would be safe, unnoticed.

Suddenly, an icy hand penetrated my cocoon. Frigid fingers caressed my hot shoulder, sending chills through my body.

A silent scream filling my head, I bolted upright, flinging back the covers. As my eyes adjusted to the darkness, my worst nightmare became a reality of horror.

I was alone.

Completely alone.

The icy hand that touched my shoulder that night long ago was the first of many incidents through the years. It occurred a few days after the death of my paternal grandmother, Fannie. Was this Grandma, telling me goodbye?

Two months later, my parents, older sister, younger brother, and I moved into the house that Grandma Fannie had shared with Gramps. On her deathbed, Grandma Fannie had declared that no one would ever be happy in that house. It was a curse we would soon remember, and never forget.

The Old Farmhouse

Gramps lived most of his childhood in an old, ramshackle farmhouse in Southwestern Pennsylvania. It was a time of enchantment and mystery. Apple orchards adjacent to the dwelling were often resting places for Gypsy caravans. The colorful wagons, seductive music, and mystical atmosphere drew the children like flies to honey. Many nights the children sat around the crackling campfires, spellbound by magical tales spun by the elders. It was the Gypsies who taught Gramps to tell fortunes by reading an ordinary deck of playing cards. In later years, he amazed friends and neighbors with the accuracy of his readings.

Great-grandma Kate, a God-fearing woman who hailed from England, was sensitive to earth bound spirits around her. She taught her children that most roaming spirits were not to be feared. Unfriendly spirits could be banished simply by asking, "What in God's name do you want?" This question was asked on many occasions in the old, dilapidated house.

Every night at precisely 10:00 p.m., the locked front door of the farmhouse would mysteriously open and close. Heads would turn as wide-eyed children fell silent and followed, with their eyes, the sound of rustling skirts crossing the room. Just as mysteriously, the door at the far end of the room would open and close.

One night, the children decided to thwart the nightly visitor. As the hands of the clock slowly moved toward 10:00, the children could hardly contain their excitement. The dim room, lit only by candles and a small fire, grew colder with each minute. The smell of the fire mixed with that of fear and anticipation. The air crackled with tension. Giggling nervously, they piled against the front door, determined to keep it from opening. Eight young bodies leaned heavily against the door and each other. Slowly, the knob turned. As the children pushed with all their might, groaning from the effort, the huge, solid wood door swung open with ease, flinging children aside as if they were light as feathers.

The sound of rustling skirts over crinolines moved slowly across the room. The children raced toward the other door. The unseen visitor hesitated not one step as bodies rushed past. From the smallest toddler to the older boys with muscles hard from working on the farm, the children toppled over each other in their haste. Bracing themselves, they were determined to keep the second door closed. Shouting encouragement, veins pumping with adrenaline, the children crowded against the wooden door. Pushing with all their might, breathing hard from the exertion, the children watched as the doorknob turned. No matter how hard they tried to keep the door closed, their efforts were fruitless. The children tumbled backwards as the door opened wide.

As they watched the door close, they shook their heads in wonder and planned for the next encounter.

The upper floor of the old farmhouse was reached by climbing a narrow, circular stairway. At the top of the stairs was a landing, with a door that opened onto a hallway. Even on the hottest days, all who crossed the threshold at the top of the stairs immediately felt a chill. Gramps compared the feeling to a cold finger being run down his spine.

The family soon got used to the creaks and groans of the big old house. The nightly visitor, the cold spot, and other unusual occurrences were eventually viewed as normal.

An old barn on the land was often a playground for the children. The smell of hay and animals long gone filled the air. Sunlight peeked through openings created by missing boards. The deep shadows provided shelter from the sun on hot days. Musty corners made perfect cover for a game of hide and seek.

One day, while digging in the dirt floor, one of the children uncovered the top of an old barrel. Eagerly the other children joined in the digging as they imagined the wonderful treasure that awaited them. Visions of gold coins, paper money, and even jewels filled their heads.

Impatiently, they pried the rotted wood from the top of the barrel. Boards creaked as rusted nails gave up their hold. The groans of disappointed children filled the hot summer air when only stacks of old, yellowed papers were revealed. As the children tossed the old papers into the air in frustration, their father came to see what all the commotion was about. Browsing through the yellow, tattered paper, he discovered that the barrel did indeed hold a treasure.

Amidst the crumbling papers was the will of a previous owner, who had died many years before. The discovery of the will ended a long-time family dispute. It did not, however, mark the end of the odd occurrences at the old farmhouse.

As Gramps matured into a young man, he followed the only course available to most men in the vicinity and became a coal miner. The hours were long, the job dirty, and the pay minimal.

Many coal miners bore visible scars of their occupation. Gramps had lost the ends of a thumb and index finger. Coupling together two cars which were used to carry the coal from the mine, his hand had been trapped when the cars shifted. Safety was not a major concern of the company bosses at that time.

The men often told tales of ghosts in the tunnels. The spirits of those miners who did not make it out were often credited with saving those who did. There was a special bond, a brotherhood of sorts, between those who spent most of their days in darkness.

Before the sun had risen on one particular day, Gramps made his way down the farmhouse steps to the kitchen below. He could hear his mother preparing breakfast and smell the aroma of fresh coffee.

Retrieving his shoes as he prepared for another day in the mines, he said good morning to his father, who sat in his regular spot at the head of the kitchen table.

Gramps bent over to tie his shoes, dreading the day to come. The back-breaking job sapped the strength right out of the body and the fatigue never seemed to leave. There were plenty of things a young man of his age would rather be doing.

"Son", his father said. "Don't go down into the hole today".

Gramps looked up in amazement, surprised that his father would advise him to miss a day of work. God knew the family needed the money.

The chair at the head of the table was empty.

It was in that instant Gramps realized he could not have seen or heard his father. His father was dead, and had been for several years.

The words of his father weighed heavy on his heart. Gramps by this time was used to unexplained events and had no doubt he had not imagined seeing and hearing his father.

Grandma Kate listened intently as Gramps relayed what had just happened.

"You know how I feel" Grandma Kate advised. "The Lord works in mysterious ways. If your Pa told you to stay home it must be for a good reason. You might want to listen to him."

Gramps took the advice of his father, but he always remembered the warning with a feeling of guilt and sadness.

The man who took Gramps' place in the mine that day lost more than a thumb or finger. He lost his life.

"Is someone there?" she asked.
Only the wind answered her call.

The Knock at the Door

Gramps met and married Fannie Cowan. Grandma Fannie, like Great-grandma Kate, was a no-nonsense, strong willed woman.

Grandma Fannie and Gramps lived with their seven children in a two-story stone house built on the bank of the Monongahela River. Thick stone walls, which kept the house cool in summer, did little to hold in the warmth in the winter. Sparsely furnished, with rooms no bigger than necessary, the house was considered regal by many people living in shanties in the nearby town.

Late one winter night, the children tucked in bed, Grandma Fannie pulled her chair closer to the fire in an effort to find some warmth. The firelight cast a soft glow over the shabby furnishings. The peace and quiet was a welcome relief from the daily clamor of such a large family. The gentle rocking of the chair lulled Grandma Fannie into a peaceful reverie.

A heavy rapping came at the door. Startled, Grandma Fannie

apprehensively made her way to the window. Company at that time of night usually meant bad news.

Frigid air had etched the window with ornate crystal designs. Softly falling snow curtained anyone who might be standing in the darkness on the other side.

Grandma Fannie moved toward the door, calling out "Who's there?" Receiving no answer, she opened the door and cautiously peered into the darkness. Seeing no one, she opened the door farther.

"Is someone there?" she asked.

Only the wind answered her call. The snow on the doorstep was undisturbed.

Thinking she must have been dreaming, she returned to her chair, pulling her shawl closer around her as she put another log on the fire.

The knocking came again, louder than before and quite insistent.

Getting a little angry, Grandma Fannie opened the heavy wooden door, ready to scold the expected prankster.

Shivering in the cold was a young man dressed in a military uniform. The soldier gazed out from the darkness with huge, sad eyes. Snow and ice clung to his clothes and clouds of breath formed as he spoke. In a weary voice he pleaded, "Tell my mother I love her."

Before she could respond, the young man disappeared before her eyes.

Grandma Fannie had no doubt regarding the identity of her

mysterious visitor. The son of a neighbor, he had been killed in the war just weeks before.

Like A Whisper

Like a whisper

A flash of light

Odd hours of the day

My dreams at night

Your image passes

In the innermost depths

Of my heart and my soul

Never giving me rest

Like a ghost roaming, floating

Thru the halls of my mind

I reach out to touch you

But once more I find

Like a soft summer breeze

Softly caressing my skin

Felt but for a moment

You've vanished again

322 Mexico Road

The house on Mexico Road was one of many in a town built to house the men who slaved in the coal mines. The company had given the families the opportunity to buy the houses, and many had been enlarged.

Gramps and Grandma Fannie, the second owners of their tiny house, had transformed the attic into two bedrooms. The narrow back porch was converted into a kitchen. Although the back of the house was two stories from the ground, they never constructed a set of stairs. The kitchen door opened to a drop of several feet. Gramps and Dad had dug out a full basement, which contained a coal room, furnace room, bathroom, and a large main area. The only way into or out of the house was through the living room or the basement.

Grandma Fannie died in the main bedroom of the house after a long illness. Not wanting to live alone, Gramps invited our family to live with him.

One sunny afternoon, not long after moving into the house, I heard my name spoken.

"Nora."

Looking up from getting a glass of water in the kitchen, I expected to see someone standing in the doorway. The voice had been soft, but clear. There was no one there.

Shrugging my shoulders, I went back to what I was doing.

"Nora."

"Just a minute!" I called back.

It was a time when people did not bother to lock their doors during the day and seldom locked them at night. It was not uncommon for friends or neighbors to walk in, calling "Anyone home?"

Walking through the dining room and into the living room, I went to see who was at the door. I stepped onto the porch, looked up and down the street. No one was in sight.

I walked back into the kitchen, thinking it must have been my imagination. It dawned on me that our dog, Toby, had not barked as he usually did when someone came into the house.

"Nora." This time the voice was louder.

"Okay, enough is enough," I fumed. Searching the house, I expected to find my sister or brother playing a trick on me.

It was a futile effort. I found no one.

Over the next 10 years, I often heard my name spoken when I was alone. It was always a female voice. Perhaps it was Grandma Fannie.

I awakened to the sound of heavy footsteps ....

Footsteps

My sister Jean and I shared the back bedroom of the converted attic. Gramps and my brother Bob shared the front. Because of the low, sloped ceiling, it was impossible to install a door between the rooms. The floor was covered with vinyl linoleum. Each room contained one electrical outlet. The only light in our bedroom came from a bed lamp affixed to the headboard of Jean's bed.

I awakened to the sound of heavy footsteps echoing eerily on the linoleum floor. Back and forth they paced, from the foot of my bed to the foot of Jean's, which could not have been more than four or five feet. Peering into the darkness, I could barely make out a shadowy form. Shaking with fear I called out, "Jean! Jean! Wake up!"

"What do you want?" was the mumbled, sleepy reply.

"Turn on the light!" I pleaded.

Angry at being wakened, Jean listened as I tearfully told of the footsteps and the shadowy figure pacing between our beds. Searching under the beds and behind the ironing caddie that held our clothes, Jean tried to convince me that I had been dreaming. The cramped room was too small to hide an intruder. Besides, someone would have to walk through the house, up the stairs, and through the front bedroom to get to our room. Not to mention also getting past our dog, Toby, whose favorite sleeping place was on the stairs.

Unconvinced, I reluctantly acknowledged she must have been right.

As Jean turned off the light, she chided me for being a scaredy cat.

Thump! Thump! Heavy footsteps echoed from out of the darkness. From Jean's bed to mine and back again, the shadowy figure paced.

Jean quickly decided that it might be best if we both slept in the same bed that night, with the light on!

Many nights, Dad and Mom would hear someone walking around upstairs. Investigation would find everyone in bed, sound asleep. We never did discover who walked the floors at night.

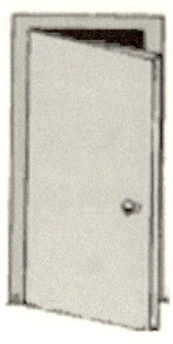

The Locked Door

Jean and I would often spend Sunday afternoon playing cards at the dining room table with our mother. We played Five Hundred Rummy and gambled with pennies in games of Poker. Mom and Jean would tease me unmercifully when I would claim threes and fives wild, giving me better odds at winning.

On this particular afternoon, Dad was taking a nap in the bedroom which opened off the dining room. It was the same bedroom in which his mother had died after her long illness.

Being a little more noisy than usual, I giggled as my pile of pennies grew. Several times, Mom reminded us to be quiet. Dad had a nasty temper, and if we awakened him there would be hell to pay for sure.

We heard a noise and looked up to see the heavy bedroom door opening slowly. It went all the way back against the wall and stayed there for several minutes.

"Uh-oh!" I groaned. "We're in trouble now!"

I thought it odd the door had opened slowly and was not yanked open in anger as expected.

"Quick, put away the cards," Mom instructed, as she grabbed up glasses of soda and plates of snacks.

My heart was pounding as I began gathering cards. Jean scooped pennies into a cloth bag. Our laughter turned to fear as we braced ourselves for the ranting and raving that was sure to come.

To our surprise, the door began to slowly swing shut. Although the door was solid wood and quite heavy, it closed rather gently. We heard the soft click as the latch fell into place.

Jean and I froze in our tracks. Walking gingerly to the door, Mom turned the knob. To her surprise, the door was locked. Dad, we later learned, had never been out of bed.

We nervously joked about the person to whom we attributed this, and many other occurrences. "It must have been Grandma."

Terror in the Night

It is not unusual for children to fight going to bed. My five-year-old brother was no different. He lay on the floor watching TV, his head nodding, as he tried in vain to keep awake. Several times he used the excuse, "I'm only resting my eyes!"

Losing her patience, Mom picked him up and set him on his feet.

"For the last time, go to the bathroom and get to bed," she admonished.

Poor Bob was so sleepy he didn't know what he was doing. My sister and I laughed as he started to pee in the corner wastebasket! But then, none of us kids would venture alone to the bathroom in the basement at night. Many times, Gramps had to go with us and wait outside the door.

Half-awake, Bob made his way up the stairs to the bedroom. As he reached the top of the stairs, he let out a blood-curdling scream! Crying hysterically, he half ran, half tumbled back down the stairs.

The whole family came running. Dad grabbed hold of Bob to keep him from running out of the house. As Mom tried to comfort him, he struggled through his tears, unable to find his voice. Finally it was understood that as he reached the top of the stairs, he looked into the back bedroom and saw something that terrified him—something that was standing at the foot of my bed.

Dad immediately went up the stairs, flipping the light on as he went. He looked high and low and found nothing out of place, no intruders. He found nothing that could have frightened Bob so badly. He also realized that Bob had seen whatever it was that terrified him in total darkness.

This incident could easily be attributed to a sleepy child's bad dream. Bob would disagree. Forty years later, he remembers the incident as clearly as if it happened yesterday.

When asked what he saw, Bob shakes his head and says he doesn't remember. He doesn't want to remember. Whatever he saw was so horrible, the terror remains in his mind to this day.

322 Mexico Road

In 1960, Grandma Fannie died in the downstairs bedroom after suffering for a year with cancer. Grandma Fannie had declared on her deathbed that no one would be happy in this house. The atrocities that occurred here were a testament to this curse.

Grandma Fannie, my father, and stepfather all died in the same room in this house, located by the window at the far right of the picture.

The top window on the left side of the house is in the room shared by my sister and me. It is the scene of the footsteps at night, and the sight of something so terrible my brother remembers the incident 45 years later, as if it happened yesterday.

Grandma Fannie

My first encounter with something I felt but could not see happened within days of Grandma Fannie's death. Was the icy hand I felt touching my shoulder my grandmother telling me goodbye?

Grandma Fannie had experienced her own ghostly encounters. When we were unable to explain strange happenings in the house at 322 Mexico Road, our first thought was usually "It's probably Grandma".

An evil woman, Grandma Fannie put a curse on the house that we soon were to remember, and never forget.

Gramps

Behind Gramps is the door that opened by itself on two occasions. It is the door to the bedroom in which three family members died.

Great-grandma Kate

Gramps' mother advised unfriendly spirits could by banished by asking "What in God's name do you want?"

Mom and Me

Mom's visit to me shortly after her death was the foundation for writing this book. She sent a message to my sister Jean, through Jean's granddaughter, on the very same day.

Dad

For months I had a recurring dream in which Dad had come back to life. In the dream I told him repeatedly that I wanted him to be around when my second child was born. I am convinced Dad let me know he was aware he had a new grandson. He also visited my Mom and brother to let them know he was still around.

Hello from Dad

My father was a man of little patience, with a terrible temper. I remember him as always yelling, seldom speaking normally. He also had a drinking problem that prevented him from taking medicine to control his high blood pressure. My mother said his temper tantrums and the physical abuse she endured began only after we moved into the house on Mexico Road. The house which his mother, on her deathbed, had declared that no one would ever be happy in. I am sure that sleeping in the bedroom where his mother had suffered and died did not help the situation.

June 1975, one week before my father's 51st birthday, he awakened at 3 a.m. Unable to breathe, and drenched in sweat, he awakened my mother and told her that he was ill and was going onto the porch for some air. Within minutes he was back. As he sat on the edge of the bed, he asked my mother for a cold cloth. Standing at the kitchen sink seconds later, she heard a thump as he fell to the floor. By

3:30 a.m., he was dead in virtually the same spot in which his mother had died 15 years before.

Several weeks later, Bob and our mother were sitting at the dining room table talking about Dad. Bob was living at home, and had tried to revive Dad on the night of his death. He and Mom were reminiscing, remembering how Dad had been talking of wanting to be cremated the very night before he died.

Bob suddenly became uneasy, feeling the hair stand up on the back of his neck. Glancing toward the bedroom, he and Mom were shocked to see the bedroom door opening on its own, as it had on that summer afternoon years before. They were stunned, to say the least, since there was no one else in the house.

In the time it would take to cross the dining room, a flower vase on the buffet suddenly toppled over for no reason.

Mom and Bob are both convinced the unseen visitor was Dad, letting them know he was still around.

Hello Again

Dad died when my older son, his only grandchild at the time, was barely three years old. Dad had adored Johnny. He often sent Johnny cigar boxes stuffed with candy and toys. Johnny's birth was the only time my father ever told me he was proud of me. As bad as he was a father, by the same degree he was a good grandfather. When Dad died, I was not sorry to lose a father, but sorry he would not see Johnny grow up

Soon after his death, I became pregnant with my second child. For months I had a recurring dream. In the dream, Dad had come back to life. He would be angry and yelling, and I would say "Daddy, settle down. If you don't, you're going to have another heart attack. I want you to be alive to see the new baby".

Easter Sunday, 1976, James Carroll came into the world. We gave him my father's middle name. Because I had a difficult pregnancy, my doctor wanted me to deliver the baby in the old hospital next to his office. The new hospital was all the way across town, with railroad tracks and heavy traffic in between. The old hospital was in good condition, but lacked many of the facilities of the newer hospital. The room I shared with another new mother did not have a private bathroom. The bathroom in the hall, outside our door, was small and stuffy. I chose to use the one down the hall, next to the nurse's station.

As I stepped from the shower the day after Jim's birth, the bathroom lights came on. I thought this was odd, since I had not heard anyone come in. Also, one-half of the outer wall was windows, which let in enough sunlight so that lights weren't necessary.

Looking under the stall doors, I did not see any feet. There were no sounds of another person in the room.

Immediately, I thought of my Dad. "That's ridiculous" I said aloud to myself. "It's just my imagination".

As the last word left my mouth, the lights went out. Walking over and flipping the lights on and off, I noticed the switch made a definite click, which I had not heard. Nothing seemed loose.

Hurrying down the long hall, I couldn't get the thought of Dad out of my head. As I breathlessly got back into bed, my roommate noticed my nervousness, and asked if I was OK.

"The strangest thing just happened" I said, relaying the dream and the incident in the bathroom.

"I couldn't help but think it was Dad, telling me he is here and knows he has a new grandson" I finished.

At that moment, the light above my bed came on. My roommate

and I looked at each other, speechless.

"Thank you Daddy" I thought, "for letting me know you are here".

"I hate to tell you this," Jean said in a shaky voice,

as I broke out in goose bumps.

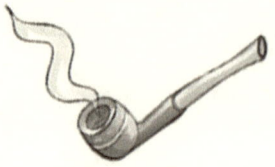

The Phone Call

Gramps was in his early 80s and in amazingly good health for a man who had spent his life working in a coal mine. He was missing the ends of a thumb and index finger, caught between the couplings of two coal cars. Like his fellow miners, he had black lung, but he never complained. He often bragged that he had never had a headache in his life. Until his 70s, when he had prostate surgery, he had not a single grey hair. His only vice was the pipe, which he smoked almost constantly. The distinct smell of Cutty Pipe tobacco lingered long after he had left a room.

As I child I listened for hours as Gramps told stories of his life growing up on the farm. He taught me to read cards as the gypsies had taught him. "If you ever meet a gypsy," Gramps instructed, "you are to say, 'Romani?' If they are not Romani, they are not true gypsy."

Mom had been shopping one Friday morning and came home to find Gramps sitting in his favorite recliner. Rubbing his stomach, he complained of not feeling well.

"Do you think you should go to the emergency room?" Mom asked.

"I think so," Gramps answered to Mom's surprise.

As they made their way to the hospital Gramps grew steadily worse, complaining of severe pain. By the time they reached the emergency entrance, Gramps was bleeding from his rectum.

Tests revealed that Gramps had an impacted bowel. Surgery was performed, but it was too late. The bowel had ruptured and poisons had spread through his body. On Saturday, the doctors gave Mom the sad news that it would be only a matter of time before Gramps died. There was nothing that could be done.

Mom's dad had died when she was 13 years old. A coal miner, he had lost a leg in an accident. Mom and my uncles often said he had died from a broken heart because he could no longer dance. Gramps was the closest thing Mom had to a father. She lovingly called him Dad. They had lived in the same house for over 20 years.

I awakened to the ringing of the telephone. Turning on the bedside light, I noticed it was 3 a.m. on Sunday. The thought entered my mind that Dad, Gramps' son, had awakened at 3 a.m. the morning he died.

"Hello?" I answered the phone, fearing the worst.

"Sorry to call you so late," was my sister's reply. "I thought you should know what is going on. Gramps is getting worse. The doctors do not think he will live another day. You'd better make plans to come home."

"How's Mom?" I asked, knowing my mother did not deal with death well. I remembered seeing my mother's unconscious body being carried into the house, after she saw Grandma Fannie in the funeral home. At Dad's funeral, she kept passing out and holding her breath. She had to be taken from the funeral home to the hospital, where she was given a shot. She remembered nothing of the funeral.

"Not good," Jean answered. "The doctors have given her a shot to calm her down. They said if she gets any worse, they are going to admit her, too."

"Oh great," I answered. "I'll be there as soon as I can."

Around 10 a.m., I called Jean to tell her the kids and I were on our way.

"Jean's at the hospital," her husband Mike told me. "Your Mom's not doing well."

"Yes, I know," I replied. "Jean told me when she called me early this morning."

Mike grew quiet and sounded strange as he said, "I'll tell Jean you're on your way."

The phone rang as I was about to go out the door.

"When did I call you?" Jean asked when I answered the phone.

"At 3 a.m.," I answered, wondering what was going on. "You said Mom wasn't doing well and the doctor's said they might have to admit her." I relayed the rest of the conversation.

"I hate to tell you this," Jean said in a shaky voice, as I broke out in goose bumps. "Everything you just said is true, but I never called you. I've been at the hospital all night."

"Oh my God," I whispered. "Then who did?"

As the smell of Cutty Pipe tobacco filled the air, I knew who had made the mysterious phone call.

Miracle in the Ashes

The house I lived in, with my husband and children, was originally meant to be a summer home. Set in the middle of the woods, the small cabin had electric baseboard heat, and a wood stove. I was afraid to go to bed with a fire in the stove, often staying up long into the night.

One morning in early January, as I backed the car to turn around on my way to work, I noticed the bright orange sun reflected in the skylights across the front of the house. "It looks just like the house is on fire," I thought out loud.

Two nights a month, I played cards with a group of friends. We took turns playing at each other's homes. That evening, the phone rang as I was telling my friends about the sun that morning, and how it looked as if the house was on fire.

"It's John", our hostess called to me. "He says it's an emergency."

Rushing to the phone, my first thought was that one of the kids was hurt. Jim tended to be accident-prone.

"You better come home", John told me breathlessly. "I brought the kids to the neighbors'. They're fine. The house is on fire!"

"Oh My God, where are my shoes and coat?" I hurriedly explained what was happening, and rushed out the door.

As I sped home I passed the fire truck, going the other way! They had run out of water and had to drive to the nearest hydrant to get more.

I could hardly get through the cars parked along the road. The throng of people watching the blaze blocked my path. What hole had these people crawled out of? We were in the middle of the country, off the main highway!

There were people sitting on tree stumps, watching my house burn down. "Get the hell off my property!" I yelled!

I found John just as my friends from the card game found me. The fire was mostly out, there was no moon, and I could not see a thing. I could smell the acrid smoke, but had no idea how bad the damage was. As my friends gathered 'round to embrace and comfort me, I sobbed.

Many, many times during my childhood, we had been awakened in a smoke filled bedroom. We would be rushed to the neighbors, where we waited anxiously for the firemen to come and put out the burning mattress in my parents' room. They had a habit of falling asleep while smoking in bed. The terror of those nights had come back big time. The difference was, this time my home was gone.

While I was out for an evening with my friends, John had taken the boys and gone for cigarettes. When he returned he found the house on fire. The culprit was the wood stove.

We collected the children and our dog from the neighbors', and spent the night in town.

The next morning, as we drove down the long dirt driveway to the cabin, I was again overcome with anguish. We had lost everything but the clothes on our backs.

I sifted through the piles of wet, burned belongings. Here was part of the Superman curtains from the boys' room. There was a portion of the trousers I had embroidered for Jimmy. It was a month after Christmas. All the children's' toys were gone.

I found a pile of ashes that had once been my jewelry box. The hinges were melted, the box was completely incinerated, but lying in the ashes was a miracle! My mother's wedding band, worn thin after more than twenty-five years on her finger, was not even melted! There were the pearl earrings Dad had given Mom for their wedding anniversary! Inside a plastic box, which had melted into a lump from the heat, was a ring, untouched. The gold locket I had received as a high school graduation present was lying in the ashes, as perfect as the day it was received.

As I stumbled around what had once been our bedroom, I discovered another miracle. Inside the closet had been a cardboard box, which held photo albums. The bedroom walls were gone; there was no longer a closet or cardboard box. In the middle of what had been the closet floor stood the pile of photo albums. As I gathered them up I thanked God for sparing what I would have most hated to lose. He had spared my children. He had spared the family treasures that were irreplaceable. When I later took the photos out of the album they were singed around the edges. The only ones I lost, about half a dozen of them, had been water damaged.

For the jewelry and photographs to have survived, in a fire hot enough to melt the telephone, was truly a miracle.

Looking for Annie

Surrounded by a beautiful, lush golf course on one side and farmland on the others, The Inn sat at the bottom of a long hill. No longer a private residence, The Inn housed overnight guests looking for the peace and quiet that could be found in the country. The former manor house boasted beautiful guest rooms decorated in period furnishings. It also had a resident ghost, affectionately named Annie by the staff.

Working at the adjacent golf course, I had become friendly with the owners, who also owned The Inn. The property manager knew that I had an interest in ghosts. He offered to let me stay in "Annie's Room" for free, to see if I could detect anything. Excited at the prospect, I asked for a tour of The Inn before I made a decision. Joining me on the private tour were several other staff members from the golf course.

As we went from room to room, we were shown the window Annie had been seen looking out of. The bathroom where she playfully kept putting the toilet seat up was just off the bedroom she favored.

We heard first-hand accounts from people who had actually seen her. She was described as a young woman, tall and dark-haired, with a mischievous temperament. She wore a white blouse and floor length dark skirt.

Hanging back from the group, I hoped to detect Annie's presence. I tiptoed to the basement, peering into the darkness. I was disappointed when I felt and saw nothing unusual.

As we were about to return to the main level of The Inn, I spotted a beautiful staircase leading up to the attic. Red-carpeted stairs rose gracefully to a small, white door set in the wall. Wanting to see every nook and cranny, I asked permission to go to the attic. The others crowded behind me as we climbed the stairs.

As soon as I began the climb, I felt heaviness settle over me. The laughter from those behind me dimmed, as if I had suddenly gone deaf. The sense of apprehension grew. The closer to the white door I got, the more afraid I became.

As I stood at the door, I put out my hand and touched the wood. Immediately such a feeling of terror overcame me, I thought I would be sick. The image of an older man flashed before me. Brown curly hair, long pork-chop sideburns, and a craggy face full of rage filled my mind. I saw him standing on the other side of the door, dressed in a dark coat and pants, a black cane with a gold top raised above his head.

"Let me through," I told the others, as I pushed my way back down the stairs. "I can't go in there."

The feeling of evil grew stronger. Whoever waited on the other side of the door did not want us in there!

"What's wrong?" the others asked. Not wanting to frighten them with details, I simply said, "I don't know what's in there, but it's not Annie."

Oblivious to what I was feeling, the others excitedly entered the attic. As I listened to the laughter and footsteps above, I quickly made my way to my car. I was 20 miles away before the feeling of evil and terror left me.

Each day as I passed The Inn on my way to work, I glanced to the attic windows. Expecting to see a craggy face looking back at me, I would feel the fear return. Needless to say, I politely turned down the offer to spend the night.

In the same instant, I realized that I did not recognize her.

Lady in the Chair

The old duplex had been converted into offices. Huge oak trees, which lined the street, provided cool shade from the hot afternoon sun. The broad front porch was perfect for rocking chairs. I imagined evenings spent there by previous inhabitants, perhaps sipping tall glasses of cold lemonade. I was soon to discover that the old house had at least one tenant who still lingered.

As I entered the front door, I stepped into a beautiful entryway. Crystal teardrops cascading from an old chandelier cast rainbows of color on the frosted inner door. Roses in the time faded wallpaper had changed to light pink in a once ivory background.

Opening the inner door, I found myself in a long hallway. To my left was an office that had once been the parlor. The comfortable furnishings gave a cozy feeling to the room. High windows, shuttered against the noise of traffic, added to the ambiance. The energy in the room felt serene, calm.

At the end of the hall, the former dining room was now a reception area. The metal filing cabinets and scuffed desk looked out of place. The large plant meant to soften the décor suffered from lack of proper lighting. Dying leaves drooped and fell to the floor. The frayed Oriental rug in the middle of the hardwood floor did little to brighten the room. Walls once a soft green were faded and in need of a fresh coat of paint. The energy here was of neglect, almost giving a feeling of sadness to anyone sensitive enough to feel it.

The old kitchen had been neglected most of all. The high ceiling was dingy and dirty, a single bulb hanging from a long cord in the center. In the far corner to the left, a door stood partly open, darkness from below spilling into the kitchen. Obviously the door to the basement, it was painted a dark green, which contrasted sharply with the dirty white walls. Looking at the door, I was surprised to feel the hair stand up on my arms. I shivered as a chill went down my back.

Quickly, I crossed the large room and pushed the door shut. Looking for a lock, I found none. Shutting the door would have to do.

The once grand staircase, now rickety and old, still exuded a touch of charm. White spindles were topped with a broad, dark banister. The worn treads evidenced the many feet that had traveled up and down the stairs through the years. At the top of the stairs, I found myself in another long hallway.

Three bedrooms had been turned into offices. A Pastoral Counselor used the first. From the middle room strains of soft music danced with aromatherapy scents used by the massage therapist. At the end of the hallway, in what had once been the master bedroom, I guided clients into hypnosis.

I had thought long and hard before renting the space here. I was concerned with the many different energy levels in the building. Going from room to room was like going from hot to cold, stormy to tranquil, calm to fear. The location was acceptable, it was easy for clients to find, and the price was right. Against my better judgment, I moved in.

I soon found that I was often alone in the old house at night. The counselors and massage therapist worked mainly days. Most of my clients preferred appointments after work. I jokingly asked the massage therapist if he heard odd noises in the house.

"Oh yes," he said nonchalantly. "It's haunted."

Tell me something I don't know, I thought.

The closet door in my office had a mind of its own. The door refused to remain closed. Each time I entered the room I would close the door firmly, turn the lock, take out the key, and pull vigorously to make sure the door was locked. Minutes later, I would hear a pop of the latch and a creak, as the old door swung open. I finally had to place a heavy piece of furniture in front of it.

The room contained my desk, an audio system, and four recliners. The Oriental rug and scattered plants added to the warmth of the room. Freshly painted walls were framed with rich, dark woodwork. The energy here was friendly and warm.

The afternoon was bright and cheery. As I entered the house, I noted that I would again be the only therapist working that night. I had several clients scheduled. As I mounted the stairs, I was mentally running through my list of things-to-do.

Opening the door to my office, I was startled to see a young woman sitting in one of the recliners. Dark hair framed a youthful face that appeared to be twenty-something. I noticed she was wearing a long sleeved white blouse, which seemed inappropriate for the hot day, over a dark short skirt.

At first I thought a client had come early, and had gone on up to my office. In the same instant, I realized that I did not recognize her. As I was about to ask if I could help her, she vanished before my eyes!

After that day, I made a point to speak to my ghostly visitor whenever I entered or left the room. I would say hello, ask that she not disturb my clients or me during the sessions, and say goodnight when I left. She never appeared again, although I felt her presence often.

When I would lock up at night, it was necessary for me to turn out the lights and leave by the back door. This meant that I would have to dash through the dark kitchen, which I feared.

I soon decided that this was not a ritual I wanted to experience on a regular basis and moved to a new location.

Not long after, the house was put up for sale. It has been on the market for several years. Perhaps prospective buyers also feel the unfriendly energy and whoever, or whatever, resides within the basement.

"Some of You Will Leave Here Changed"

"During the next week, you will each be both the therapist and the client. You will confront your past, heal old wounds, and clear blockages. Some of you will go home a changed person. You will need to adjust, and your families will need to adjust. It won't be easy."

The instructor's words cut through me like a knife.

Oh no, I thought to myself. *I don't know if this is a good thing.*

I had come to the remote bed and breakfast for a week-long class. At the end of the class, if I passed, I would be well on my way to being certified as a Master Hypnotherapist. This class was just beginning, but it was already intriguing!

Nine strangers, who had come together from all over the country, were about to experience one of the most intensive weeks of their lives - a week that would leave many changed forever. Jaycea was from Texas, Dale and Lillian from Canada, Susan was from New Mexico, and some others and I were from the East coast. Our group was comprised of a doctor, a social worker, hypnotherapists, massage therapists, psychics, and an EMT. We had full time practices and part-time practices. We were young and older, male and female. We were different but alike. By the end of the week, we would be friends.

We learned advanced methods of hypnosis, deepening techniques, reframing and regression methods. We were both student and teacher. We helped others heal emotionally, and found ourselves healed. We remembered things long forgotten. We learned things we would never forget. We learned about emotional clearing, regression language, experienced our own regressions, and guided others through their regression experiences. Each day, we learned a new technique involving regression therapy. Some were past life, some the past of this life. We never knew where the subject of the demonstration would go as Allen, our instructor, directed him or her to "go to the source."

The final day of class was focused on physical healing. Allen had asked Dale if he would volunteer for this demonstration. Dale was an EMT and came to most of the classes wearing a back brace. Hurt on the job for the second time, he had been on disability for 18 months. He was in near constant pain, with no end in sight.

Dale gingerly climbed on top of the massage table set in the center of the room. Allen was seated at the head of the table. The rest of the class filled the circle of chairs around Dale.

As we grew quiet, one of the women picked up a crystal and laid it on Dale's body directly below the breastbone, where he had been experiencing a pinching sensation. Allen asked Dale if this was okay and he said yes, it was fine. The only one more surprised than Dale was Jaycea, who'd had the urge to place the crystal upon him.

"Okay now, as you close your eyes take a slow, deep breath," Allen began. For the next several minutes, his soothing voice guided Dale through progressively deeper levels of relaxation. As Dale passed from one stage of hypnosis to another, his body became limp. His breathing was so shallow it was almost undetectable. Allen directed Dale to "go to the source of your problem."

The class, as if one body, leaned in closer to hear his answer. I could feel the tension in the air as Dale began to breathe heavily, his expression changing from peaceful relaxation to one of anxiety. In a soft voice, he began to haltingly tell us what he was aware of.

"There are a lot of people here... I'm on a horse... I get knocked off the horse... Someone is dragging me across the ground... They throw me against a wall, and I'm left there to die."

I looked at the faces around me. I saw reflections of my own sadness, as we all pictured the scene Dale had just described.

"Tell the story again, this time with more detail," Allen instructed.

As Dale described the scene again, he was in obvious pain. He struggled to get the words out; long pauses punctuated the end of each sentence. Tears were running down his cheeks.

"There's Royalty here..... I don't have a good feeling about this...... The man I am supposed to fight is a lot younger...... He's killed over a hundred men..... I'm on the horse and he runs the lance through me."

He pointed to the spot where he had the pinching. It was exactly where Jaycea had laid the crystal!

"He knocks me off my horse...... They drag me through the dirt and leave me to die."

I glanced over at Jaycea, and saw that she, too, had tears flowing down her cheeks. Her face was a portrait of pain and grief.

Ah ha! I thought. *She was there, too! That's how she knew where to place the crystal.* Was she his girlfriend? His wife?

Allen did a check of anxiety and determined that Dale needed to go through the story again.

As he began again, Dale was in obvious agony.

"Somebody is going to die today," he whispered in a voice filled with grief.

Jaycea got up and started walking out of the room, sobbing. As a man named Bruce took her arm, she collapsed and had to be helped out.

Unaware of what was happening with Jaycea, Dale again went through the memory.

"The man who killed me is laughing about it with his friend."

This time he came to a startling realization.

"It was just a game! We died for a game!" These words were spoken in a whisper of disbelief and bewilderment. The anxiety and fear were no longer in his voice. Allen did an anxiety check and determined that Dale had reached the period of transition. Allen gave Dale the necessary hypnotic instructions and guided him back to full consciousness.

Dale jumped off the table and danced around, pain free. People immediately surrounded Dale, giving him hugs. As my turn came, he noticed that everyone was rushing out of the room.

"Where is everyone going?" he asked in confusion.

"I think you need to talk with Jaycea."

We found her sitting on a couch in the lobby, surrounded by classmates. Her mascara smeared down to her chin, her face swollen with tears, Jaycea looked as if she had gone through hell and back. As Dale sat down beside her, she put her arms around him and began to sob.

"I'm sorry! I'm so sorry!"

As Dale described his memory, Jaycea realized that she, too, had been there. She had been the man who had killed Dale. At almost the same instant that he came to his startling realization Jaycea, who was in another room, was saying in deep despair, "It was just a game. We died for a game."

What of Bruce, the man who helped her out of the room? He had been there, too. He had been the friend to whom Jaycea had bragged about killing Dale.

Three strangers, Dale from Canada, Jaycea from Texas, and Bruce from Virginia, had come together for healing and forgiveness.

Two years later, Dale was still pain free. He has a full time hypnosis practice, helping others heal, as he was healed.

As I drove home the next morning, I thought about all I had learned. I thought about the sessions I had taken part in, the laughter, the tears, and the weight that seemed to be lifted. I thought about all the wonderful people I had met, and how we each had felt so comfortable right from the start. It was as if we had all known one another before. Perhaps, in other lifetimes, we had.

"Forever" Friends

I've never gazed
Into your eyes,
Walked holding your hand
Under sun lit skies.

Kissed your face filled with laughter
Or wet with tears,
In good times and bad times
Only true friends can share.

Nor heard you whisper my name
While holding me tight,
As day slowly fades
Into star filled night.

Never caressed your brow
Watching you dream,
Your body softly bathed
In pale moonbeams.

Not in this lifetime
Tho I know 'tis true,
You've known me before
As I've known you.

I feel your presence
Tho we are apart,
Filled up with your essence
Overflowing my heart.

Fate brought us together
Let us question not,
Just embrace the moment
With all that we've got.

This bond that is between us
Doesn't need a name,
Whether soul mate or friend
The yearning is the same.

On gossamer wings of angels
You come to me in dreams,
Flickering memories of other lifetimes
Dancing with those yet to be.

Happy in My Blue Heaven

After the death of my father and grandfather, Mom spent many years living alone in the house on Mexico Road. Whenever I would visit, I often slept on the couch, wanting to avoid the upstairs bedroom. As a child, I slept surrounded by dolls and stuffed animals, hoping that whatever came to visit in the night would not know which one was me. As an adult, whenever it was necessary to sleep in the back bedroom, I would leave the light on. My sister, brother, and I avoided discussing odd occurrences in front of Mom, not wanting to frighten her.

Mom became ill, needing constant care. We sadly signed her into a nursing home. For nearly three years, we watched as her health deteriorated. In the beginning, we would take her on excursions to the mall, drives in the mountains, or out to dinner. As she became weaker and confined to a wheelchair, the trips were limited to sitting outside in the fresh air.

The saddest moment came when I called her on her birthday

and she did not recognize me. She often confused me for my sister when I called, but this day she did not know me even after I told her who I was.

A tracheotomy made it increasingly difficult for Mom to speak. As her mind wandered, she would often start a sentence only to forget what she wanted to say. As she grew weaker, she lacked the strength needed to speak. We halfheartedly joked as we tried to read her lips. Mom would become frustrated when we could not understand her, so we would just smile and nod. Sometimes she would roll her eyes and laugh, and we would know we had made the wrong response and laugh along with her.

Thanksgiving 2001 was a difficult time for us all. Mom was too fragile to leave the nursing home for dinner at my sister's. My brother and I, living several states away, were not able to get time off from work to make the trip home. That evening, we learned that Mom had retired to her room after dinner and had died.

At Mom's funeral, I spoke about my belief that we never die, although the body has been shed. I shocked Mom's minister when I said that my mother was not lying in the casket. The body is just a vehicle. The soul is eternal. My mother was not dead; she just had a new address. I read an excerpt from "The Little Soul and the Sun." I shocked several family members by being a pallbearer. I shocked them even more by having a Polka, Mom's favorite music, played as mourners filed past the casket for a final goodbye. Her brother, a former minister, kept shaking his head and saying, "I thought she was kidding. I really thought she was kidding!" I like to think Mom was watching, and smiling. She might even have been dancing the Polka in the aisles!

At work a few weeks later I was having a bad day, missing Mom terribly. I struggled to hold back the tears. I found myself humming a tune, over and over. I could not place it, but it was hauntingly familiar. Suddenly, thoughts of Mom filled my mind. I saw her smiling, in good health. I felt peace settle over me, as the words to the tune became clear.

When Whippoorwills call

And evening is night

I hurry to my blue heaven

A turn to the right

A little white light

Will lead you to my blue heaven

Just Molly and me

And baby makes three

We're happy in my blue heaven

This old song was one of mom's favorites.

"She said to tell you she's all better now," said the small voice from the back seat.

Jeannie Mae

My great-niece Alicia, who I nicknamed Jeannie Mae after my sister and me, was very close to my mother. After Mom's death, Jeannie Mae would tell her mother and grandmother that she was mad because Grandma Thelma had died. Taking Jeannie Mae to visit Mom's grave, her mother tried to explain that Grandma Thelma was in heaven now.

Jeannie Mae needed to have dental surgery. Because she was only four years old, it was decided that she needed to go to the hospital and be put to sleep for the surgery.

It was 5:00 in the morning. The sun had not yet risen as my sister drove her daughter and granddaughter to the hospital. Strapped securely in her car seat, Jeannie Mae was thought to be asleep.

"She said to tell you she's all better now," said the small voice from the back seat.

"What?" asked my sister, not sure she had heard correctly.

"She said to tell you she's all better now," Jeannie Mae said softly.

"Who?" Jean asked, in her heart already knowing the answer.

"Grandma Thelma," came the sleepy reply.

"Oh, are you talking to her?" Jean asked.

"No," Jeannie Mae said, yawning. "She's talking to me."

Arriving home later that day, Jean found a ring that had belonged to Mom lying on the porch, in front of the door. It had mysteriously disappeared soon after Mom died.

Even more surprising, Jeannie Mae and I received our messages from Mom on the very same day.

The Bed and Breakfast

On the edge of the George Washington National Forest sits the beautiful old Warm Springs Inn. Huge trees surround the main building, hanging baskets of flowers decorating the lower limbs. Ornamental geese parade across grounds bordered by shrubbery and huge bushes of flowers. Cats and kittens chase butterflies across the grass. A beautiful red and brown collie greets arriving guests. Across the street, white circular structures designed by Thomas Jefferson surround healing baths once sacred to the Indians, and a place of truce during the Civil War.

The main building, its green awning shading steps leading to the front door, had once been a courthouse. The parlor, filled with antiques cozily nestled with dime store figurines and trinkets, is a sight to behold. A beautiful crystal chandelier softly casts a warm glow over the room. The dining room, bar, and closed-in porch where breakfast is served are equally overflowing with collectibles and equally charming. The second floor of the main building is closed to the public.

The Warm Springs Inn boasts several buildings, which house guests. All are decorated in the same haphazard, charming manner as the main building. The most interesting of the buildings sports a hand-lettered sign at the crest of wide stairs leading to the front door – "The Jail." Two stories tall with a wraparound porch, The Jail is situated back from the main building, almost to itself. Sitting in one of the many rocking chairs, feeling the gentle breeze and listening to the deep country sounds, visitors have a clear view of the lovely grounds, the healing baths, and the old "hanging tree." The tree is deeply scarred on one side. The wound, we were told, is from being struck by lightening.

For several years, Jean and I had taken a "girls only" vacation together. I decided The Warm Springs Inn would be the perfect spot for our next trip. We arrived at the Inn on Friday afternoon. On a previous visit, I had picked out the room I wanted for us. The room was located at the back of The Jail, on the first floor. I specifically asked for the room by number when I made our reservation.

"Are you sure you don't want another room?" the manager asked beseechingly. "I can give you a room with double beds, or one with a twin bed and a double bed. You would be more comfortable."

"No," I insisted. "I've already looked at this room. It's the prettiest, and I want it."

Again the manager tried to direct us to other quarters. Being stubborn, I refused to change rooms. I was to find out later that he wanted us to move because we were the only living residents in The Jail that night.

Apprehensively, Jean trailed behind as we followed the manager to our room in The Jail. We entered a dim hall, the only light shed by a single lamp in the middle of an old table near the front door. The doors to the guest rooms stood open wide. We glanced in each as we passed. The stairs to the second floor rose into darkness. I had to admit the place was spooky, even in the middle of the day.

Decorated in shades of peach, our room contained two twin size beds. Huge double windows overlooked an ancient cemetery. A cow could be heard mooing in the distance.

"See," I said to Jean, faking a calmness I did not feel. "This is pretty nice."

Taking soft drinks and snacks, we went to the front porch and plopped into the rocking chairs. We were tired after our long drive, but too excited to sleep. I pointed out the hanging tree and the healing baths across the street. As the sun went down and dusk began to fall, the air grew chilly. We pulled our sweaters tighter around us.

"Do you see what I see?" Jean asked nervously.

The lights on the second floor of the main building were blinking off and on. As we watched, something seemed to float back and forth behind the window.

"What IS that?" I asked, trying to make out the shape.

As we realized what we were seeing, we broke down in nervous laughter, tears running down our cheeks. The floating object was the owner's pet monkey, swinging on a rope! As he swung back and forth, he would flip the lights on and off.

As it grew darker, we decided we would rather be behind a locked door than out on the porch in the middle of nowhere. We walked down the long hall to our room. Shadows danced on the wall from the dim light cast on huge pieces of antique furniture. We walked a little faster than necessary, glancing over our shoulders along the way. We were suddenly very aware that we were the only people in the old building. We hurried past dark rooms with doorways resembling mouths opened wide, half expecting something to reach out and grab us.

As we got ready for bed, we avoided any mention of things that go bump in the night. Not wanting to sleep in total darkness, I chose to leave the bathroom light on, making the excuse that we would need to see if we had to use the facility during the night.

Settling down beneath the heavy blankets, Jean was floating in that wonderful place between awake and asleep. Suddenly, she felt something land hard on the foot of her bed. Thinking we had left a window open and one of the many cats had gotten in, she started to get up and chase it back outside. The blankets flew over her head, stopping her in surprise. Feeling the panic rise in her throat, she tried to call out but found she was not able to speak. Frantically, she yanked the blankets down and was greeted by an unbelievable sight.

Sound asleep in the next bed, I was not aware of the soft, purple light floating above me. As Jean watched, speechless, the light seemed almost to pulsate as it glowed in the darkness. Hovering above me the light glided back and forth, up and down, as if dancing. The light grew dimmer and dimmer, until it was no more.

Surprised that her fear had left the moment she had seen the light, Jean lay back down and promptly fell asleep.

Hearing the tale the next morning, I was greatly disappointed that I had missed the whole thing. I had planned on scaring Jean, but wanted to wait until our second night. I was afraid that if I scared her on the first night, she would insist on going home. Since someone had beaten me to it, I decided to make my move.

As we started to leave for breakfast, I stood back and let Jean open the door. As I looked into the hall, I let out a gasp and jumped back. Jerking around, Jean saw there was nothing in the hall.

"#%!*#." Jean laughed as she swatted at me.

We were both glad to see other guests checking into The Jail that day. One night alone in the building was enough for both of us!

"Jesus! Jesus! Jesus! Jesus!" I screamed aloud.

The Whirling Dervish

My son John and I had made plans to visit The Warm Springs Inn. I had told him the many things that friends and I had experienced there. He was anxious to see if he, too, could pick up some lingering energy of those who had come before us.

As I told other friends about our plans, our party grew from two to seven. We arrived at the inn on Saturday afternoon, planning to have a séance later that night. We all had connecting rooms in The Jail except for John, who chose to stay on the second floor alone. My friend Karen and I stayed in the room that the manager had half-jokingly admitted to being haunted.

After an hour in the healing baths, we went out for dinner. Arriving back at the inn we were all in high spirits. Some were excited about the proposed séance, some were non-believers, and some were not so sure they wanted to participate. We lit candles and smudged the room and each other with burning sage while murmuring prayers. I let everyone know they were free to leave if they chose. Everyone stayed. The scent of incense filled the room as lights were turned down low. We sat in a circle on the floor, holding hands. I explained how we would proceed, asked everyone to close their eyes, and began to pray. As I asked for protection for those present, I could feel the air in the room grow heavy. The air suddenly felt cool. As I concluded the prayer, I felt a sadness fall over me like a cloak. Tears began streaming down my face. I felt silent sobs racking my body.

"I'm so sad. I feel an aching in my chest, like my heart is breaking. Catherine, this has to do with you. You've been here before."

I opened my eyes and saw six pairs of eyes staring back at me in surprise.

"Would you consider doing a regression?" I asked Catherine.

"Sure," she readily answered. Catherine was very knowledgeable and had no fear in being regressed.

We moved the beds apart, put a pillow on the floor in the middle of our circle, and Catherine got comfortable. I placed Catherine in a hypnotic trance, surrounded her with the white light of protection, and guided her back through time.

"Tell me what you are aware of."

"I'm a young girl.... I'm hiding in the water.... I'm looking between some boards and I see boots passing by.... Lots of boots... There is someone hiding with me."

"Who is with you?"

"They can't find him!" Catherine whispered, as tears began to slide down her cheeks. "He's black."

Her body began to tremble as she lay on the floor.

"Okay, Catherine. I'm going to count to three, and I want you to go to the next significant event. One... two... three. Tell me what you are aware of."

"We're in the cemetery... I feel a great sadness... He was caught and hanged."

"Do you want to go on?"

"No!"

Guiding her back, I instructed her to leave all the feelings of fear and sadness in the past. She would remember everything she had experienced, but she would feel calm and peaceful.

As she opened her eyes, Catherine let out a huge sigh.

There were lots of questions from the others. They asked her how she felt, if she had any idea who she and the other person had been, and what else she remembered.

We finally decided we'd had enough for one night. After blowing out the candles, each couple retired to their respective rooms.

I have no idea how long I had been asleep. I opened my eyes, shocked to see what appeared to be a small tornado spinning in the middle of the room. It was about five feet off the ground. On top of the tornado was the head of an old hag. Eyes blazing, mouth open as if in a silent scream, the hag had a huge crooked nose like that of a witch. As I watched in horror, the tornado flew at me. I was under attack! The word "dervish" entered my mind as I felt the impact.

"Jesus! Jesus! Jesus! Jesus!" I screamed aloud. As the last "Jesus!" left my lips, the tornado disappeared.

My roommate slept soundly, the night mask still covering her eyes, oblivious to what had just happened. I couldn't believe my yelling had not wakened her!

Staggering to the bathroom, I splashed cold water on my face. My body felt frozen, my teeth chattered. I got an extra blanket from the closet and climbed back into bed, sure I would not sleep any more that night.

At breakfast the next morning, my companions were spellbound as I told them what had happened.

"We heard you yelling Jesus," Catherine and her mother told me.

"Why didn't you come to see what was happening?" I asked incredulously.

"And go back into that room in the middle of the night? No way!"

So much for safety in numbers!

As the others packed to leave, I walked out to the porch of The Jail to take some video shots. As I raised the camera to my eyes, I saw jagged, wavy lines. It looked like the television screen when the stations do not come in clearly.

"Now what's wrong?" I asked myself in frustration.

To my surprise, the camera was in the "off" mode. As I moved further from The Jail, the static lines began to clear. As I moved closer to The Jail, they got worse. Moving to the edge of the property, I took a video of the grounds, the buildings, and the "hanging" tree. The camera seemed to work fine.

Viewing the tape at home, not one shot was clear. All that was visible was jagged, wavy lines. Interior shots, taken the day before, also could not be seen. Like the equipment used to record the hypnosis training sessions held there, the camera had malfunctioned. Or had it?

The camera worked perfectly before our trip and continued to work perfectly once we left the grounds of the Bed & Breakfast.

"Wait 'til you see what happens next," I heard loud and clear.

Become As Children

They say that babies who smile in their sleep are communicating with angels. Children often pick out imaginary playmates in family albums, knowing unexplainably names and other details of deceased family members.

My son John was a very bright and unusually happy child. On several occasions, he saw people that I could not see. He also had an imaginary playmate.

My niece Michele would stand in the back hall of her parents' house, looking up as if at someone taller than she, and carry on a one-sided conversation. When asked to whom she was talking, the three-year-old would only say "the man." Her daughter, Alicia, also spoke to "the man" in the hall when she was a toddler.

Through the years, I have had many experiences that could not be explained. Some were alone, some witnessed by others. Stopping my car for no apparent reason, I watched a car come around a sharp curve, cross the road directly in front of me, and crash into a tree. I have awakened in the middle of the night, heard a voice speak my name, and received a message. Two weeks later the message came true. Several weeks before hurricane Katrina, I told my family members and a friend that I felt an unusual sense of fear.

"I never feel afraid, but I have for days. I don't know what's going to happen, but it's going to be big. A lot of people are going to be hurt. I don't think it's going to be another terrorist attack."

In the aftermath of Katrina, in the middle of the night, I heard a disembodied male voice.

"Wait 'til you see what happens next," I heard loud and clear. What happened next was hurricane Rita.

I firmly believe there is much we do not see, only because we fail to look. There is much we do not hear, only because we fail to listen. There is much we do not feel, only because we do not pay attention.

It is said that children are born with the ability to see, hear, and remember what we have long forgotten.

Become as children.

Sit in the stillness.

Open your heart, your ears, and your mind.

There is another world waiting for you, if you will only take the time to pay attention.

~ Namaste' ~

"The Divine in me blesses and honors the Divine in you."

www.ingramcontent.com/pod-product-compliance
Lightning Source LLC
Chambersburg PA
CBHW020339290526
45785CB00005B/2096

* 9 7 8 1 4 1 1 6 6 2 4 5 2 *